CITIES OF THE WORLD

CHICAGO

BY R. CONRAD STEIN

CHILDREN'S PRESS®
A Division of Grolier Publishing
New York London Hong Kong Sydney
Danbury, Connecticut

CONSULTANTS

Edward K. Uhlir, F.A.I.A.
Director of Research and Planning
Chicago Park District

Linda Cornwell
Learning Resource Consultant
Indiana Department of Education

Project Editor: Downing Publishing Services
Design Director: Karen Kohn & Associates
Photo Researcher: Jan Izzo

LIBRARY OF CONGRESS CATALOGING-IN-PUBLICATION DATA

Stein, R. Conrad.
     Chicago / by R. Conrad Stein.
        p. cm. — (Cities of the world)
     Includes index.
     Summary: Describes the history, people, and places of the nation's third largest city.
     ISBN 0-516-20301-0 (lib.bdg.)   0-516-26143-6 (pbk.)
     1. Chicago (Ill.)—Juvenile literature. [1. Chicago (Ill.)]
     I. Title. II. Series: Cities of the world (New York, N.Y.)
     F548.33.S45   1997   96-9663
     977.3'11—dc20   CIP
                                                AC

TABLE OF CONTENTS

Buckingham Fountain shoots a spout of water 150 feet into the skies above Chicago. On summer evenings, colored floodlights turn the waters into a fantastic rainbow. The fountain has been called Chicago's front door. It gushes from Grant Park, the city's front yard. What a front door! What a front yard!

East of Grant Park spreads Lake Michigan. Winds sometimes howl off this huge lake. White-capped waves crash over its shores. In many ways, Lake Michigan has the look and feel of an ocean. This gorgeous lake belongs to all Chicagoans. A broad patch of parkland stretches 24 miles along the lakeshore. No other waterfront city in America has so much of its shoreline devoted to public parks.

To the west rises the skyline of downtown Chicago. Here, glimmering office towers pierce the sky. The forest of buildings reminds the world that the skyscraper was a Chicago invention. Downtown is also Chicago's historic heart. More than 200 years ago, a French-speaking black man named Jean Baptiste Point du Sable built a cabin near the mouth of the Chicago River at

Below left: Boaters setting off from Ohio Street Beach have a spectacular view of the Chicago skyline, including the John Hancock Building (center).

What's in a Name? Chicago

Chicago was once home to the Pota-watomi Indians. They called the sluggish river that flowed into Lake Michigan the *Checagou.* There is a lively debate over the meaning of that Potawatomi word. To some scholars it means "great." Others claim it means "wild onion place" because of the onions that once grew along the riverbank. Still other historians say the word means "big stink," the stink coming from rotting onions. Chicagoans are not fond of the "big stink" interpretation.

Buckingham Fountain (left) is especially beautiful during summer evenings when families like the one pictured below come to enjoy the fountain's laser light show.

Lake Michigan. Du Sable was Chicago's first non-Indian settler. Millions of others followed.

Chicagoans today hail from every point on the globe. The city's restaurants serve exotic dishes ranging from Persian shish kebabs to tangy enchiladas with the flavors of Mexico. It is a town of writers, artists, sports figures, and hardworking men and women.

And this fabulous city welcomes you through Buckingham Fountain, its front door.

Enchilada

Chicago, Chicago,
   that toddlin' town!
Chicago, Chicago,
   I'll show you around.

Let a Chicagoan show you around the city, as the line from the "Chicago Song" suggests. Your tour will probably start downtown. The city's central core is called the "Loop." It gained that nickname because the elevated train track—the L—loops around it. Those great iron L tracks were built in the 1890s. Today, the downtown area sprawls well beyond the area that was created by the tracks. No matter, downtown is still the Loop.

LOOPING THE LOOP

The mile-long section of Michigan Avenue north of the Chicago River is nicknamed the "Magnificent Mile." This is the tourists' Chicago. Some 8 million people visit the city each year. Many of them enjoy strolling along the Magnificent Mile. Lining the street are some of the city's most elegant hotels, shops, and restaurants. Jewelry and fashion stores operate near the Magnificent Mile. The stores sell items such as women's dresses worth a thousand dollars and diamond rings valued at half a million. Nearby is a recently developed neighborhood called "River North." Once an area of drab warehouses, River North is now home

Chicagoans, including the women shown at the left, enjoy shopping at exclusive Oak Street boutiques and the elegant stores that line the Magnificent Mile (above).

An aerial view of North Michigan Avenue

to some of the city's finest art galleries and trendiest restaurants.

West of Michigan Avenue is State Street. This historic street gave rise to another line in the Chicago song: "On State Street, that great street . . ." In the 1890s, a merchant named Marshall Field built a new department store on State Street. It featured skylights to make the inside bright and attractive. Before Field's time, department stores were humdrum places where clerks were gruff with customers. Field once spotted a store clerk arguing with a woman shopper. He broke up the argument by telling the clerk, "Give the lady what she wants." Forever after, that statement became the store's motto. In its glory days, State Street was lined with shopping palaces owned by merchant kings such as Field, Montgomery Ward, Richard Sears, and Alvah Roebuck. Today, only Marshall Field's and its neighboring department store, Carson Pirie Scott, survive as reminders of State Street's past splendor. Chicago's finest department stores are now found along the Magnificent Mile. State Street as "that great street" remains only in the memory of older Chicagoans.

Marshall Field's Frango mint candy

11

Farther west is La Salle Street, Chicago's financial headquarters. There, in a huge room at the Board of Trade Building, speculators shout out orders for pork bellies, bushels of grain, and other farm products. The speculators buy and sell on paper only. Most have never in their lives seen a bushel of grain or a pork belly. Yet their passion is so great, one would think they were buying and selling pure gold. The rest of La Salle Street is lined with banks and stock exchanges. It is the nerve center for Chicago's financial world.

Right: The Chicago Board of Trade Building
Below: The hectic trading floor of the Chicago Mercantile Exchange

On the northern edge of the Loop flows the Chicago River. It runs out of Lake Michigan, the reverse direction of most rivers. In the year 1900, engineers made the river flow backward to reduce the pollution of Lake Michigan. At the time, the river was crowded with cargo boats of all descriptions. Because of the dense river traffic, Chicago had more drawbridges than any other city in the world. The bridges remain, but today the river carries mainly pleasure craft and glass-topped boats crammed with tourists.

This aerial view of the Chicago River at Wacker Drive shows only a few of the many bridges that cross the river along its course.

A Swim in the River

Years ago, raw sewage and industrial waste were routinely dumped into the Chicago River. The same river where the Potawatomis once got their drinking water was reduced to a stinking sewer. But antipollution laws passed in the 1950s and 1960s sparked a great cleanup campaign. Today, 32 species of fish live in the Chicago River. Health authorities have even cleared parts of the river for swimming, although very few Chicagoans have taken the plunge.

THE SIDES — CHICAGO'S MANY WORLDS

Every business day, the Loop fills with 400,000 people who come there to work or to shop. At the end of the day, Chicagoans return to their neighborhoods, the "sides." The North Side is north of the Loop, the West Side is to the west, and the South Side lies south of downtown. Chicago has no East Side because Lake Michigan sprawls along its eastern edge.

The sides have vastly different personalities. Generations ago, Germans, Poles, and Scandinavians settled on the North Side; African Americans on the South Side; and Italians, Slavs, Greeks, and Jews on the West Side. Thus, the three sides developed like separate cities with separate identities. In the old days, some Chicagoans claimed that they could trace a person's side of town by the sound of the spoken accent. Industries further encouraged the distinctions among the sides. The West Side was once home to the giant International Harvester Company, which made farm equipment. The South Side held the stockyards, where each year millions of pigs and steers were slaughtered.

The Mexican Independence Day Parade is held every year on September 16.

This young girl attends the Ukranian Saturday School.

Far left: A German butcher displays home-made sausages at the Paulina Market, a German butcher shop.
Left: A member of a marching band that was part of the annual State Street Christmas Parade

Then, ethnic patterns changed. Blacks replaced whites on the West Side. Mexicans settled on the Near South Side, close to the Loop. Asians moved into the Near South Side and the North Side. The stockyards transferred their operations to Kansas. Other industries also left town. Old factory buildings on the North Side are now apartment lofts and studios for artists. But some things don't change. South Side baseball fans cheer for the White Sox; North Siders root for the Cubs.

Boasting about one's neighborhood is a time-honored Chicago custom. South Siders laud the University of Chicago, which has produced more Nobel Prize winners than any other such institution in the world. The Du Sable Museum of African American History is another proud South Side establishment. North Siders point to the Gold Coast and to North Lake Shore Drive. These are Chicago's wealthiest neighborhoods. West Siders talk of progress and hope for the future. The West Side contains Chicago's poorest neighborhoods. But exciting new construction projects have brightened West Side prospects.

White Sox tickets

PARKS

Parks are Chicago's lungs. They are places to breathe, play softball, take long walks, or just relax on a bench. Chicago has 542 parks that cover almost 7,500 acres. This wealth of parkland is largely the legacy of an architect and city planner named Daniel Burnham. Burnham arrived in Chicago in 1855, when he was nine years old. He became a city planner at a time when Chicago was undergoing rapid growth. As the city expanded, Burnham strongly endorsed the idea that new neighborhoods be graced with parks and that outlying areas retain forest preserves. Not all of Burnham's recommendations were realized, but his stamp remains on many of the city's magnificent green areas.

Grant Park (below) draws people all summer long for various activities that include free concerts, the Taste of Chicago food fest, and blues, jazz, and gospel festivals. Soccer (right) has become a popular spring and summer sport in parks throughout the city.

Left: Visitors to this park, with its flower garden and fountain, have a wonderful view of the John Hancock Building.

Below: A man on stilts dressed as Uncle Sam attracted a lot of attention at the Taste of Chicago, which is held during weeklong Fourth of July festivities.

These children are petting a calf at a petting zoo that is one of the many attractions at the Taste of Chicago.

Lincoln Park on the North Side is the second largest urban park in the United States. It is also one of the city's most popular parks. It lies between the lakeshore and rows of stunning apartment buildings. Lincoln Park features the Montrose Avenue Beach, the North Avenue Beach, and the Lincoln Park Zoo. The zoo is Chicago's second most-visited institution. Hugging the lakefront on the South Side is Jackson Park. A delicate Japanese garden is one of Jackson Park's landmarks. On the West Side are a series of parks: Humboldt Park, Garfield Park, and Douglas Park. These parks date to 1869.

Paddleboaters on Lincoln Park Lagoon take advantage of the summer weather.

Young and old alike enjoy visiting Lincoln Park Zoo. When walking through the animal exhibits becomes tiring, there's always a handy bench to sit on and popsicles to eat.

They are enriched with statues, gardens, lagoons, and groves of stately trees.

Few other cities have so much land dedicated to parks as does Chicago. Certainly, not all of the parks were planned decades ago by the farsighted Burnham. But the green islands enjoyed by Chicagoans today reflect Burnham's philosophy: "Make no small plans; they have no magic to stir men's souls."

A phoenix is a bird written about in Egyptian and Greek mythology. The magical bird died by bursting into flames. Then, miraculously, it soared out of its own ashes with renewed life. Chicago also suffered a death by fire. And, like the phoenix, it amazed the world by springing to life from its ashes.

A NEW CITY

Chicago began as a cabin built by Du Sable. From this cabin, Du Sable traded goods with the Potawatomi Indians. A terrible battle between American soldiers and the Potawatomi Indians was fought in frontier Chicago in 1812. It was called the Fort Dearborn Massacre. Survivors of the battle formed a new community. By 1837, Chicago had 4,000 residents, and was incorporated as a city. Just ten years later, it was a bustling boomtown, boasting 450 stores and almost 17,000 people. Location keyed

Top: Mrs. Heald, the wife of the fort's commander, fought bravely during the 1812 Fort Dearborn Massacre and managed to survive.
Above: Fort Dearborn as it looked in 1803, before it was burned down during the massacre

The Old Water Tower, in the center of this picture, was a landmark even in the 1850s.

its growth. Situated in the heart of the Midwest, the town on Lake Michigan was a natural shipping point for farm goods heading to eastern cities. In turn, plows and other machinery were shipped through Chicago to midwestern farms. During the 1850s, railroads enhanced Chicago as a shipping and warehousing giant. Between 1860 and 1870, its population swelled from 100,000 to 300,000.

Never before had a city expanded so fast. But Chicago paid a price for its runaway growth. Houses were made of wood, many of them hammered together in less than a week. The people walked on wooden sidewalks. Even some of the streets were paved with wooden bricks. The dominance of wood made early Chicago a tinderbox. In dry months, roaring fires often devoured two or three city blocks.

Sand sculpture of the Water Tower

THE CHICAGO FIRE

The fall of 1871 was rainless for many weeks. On the night of October 8, a fire started at the O'Leary barn on DeKoven Street. In the years to come, generations of Chicagoans grew up believing the fire was caused by a cow kicking over a lantern. However, Mrs. O'Leary later swore in court that she had no lantern in her barn that evening. Soon, orange flames licked over the O'Leary barn and spread to a shed next door. Initially, it seemed that another one of Chicago's all too frequent local fires had broken out. However, the firemen went to the wrong location at first. That gave the blaze extra time to catch hold. Then the wind whipped up over the prairies outside of town, fanning the flames. The blaze became a monster. "The devil's own fire," said one fireman.

Driven by a now howling wind, the flames advanced from the South Side toward downtown. Some witnesses said the fire moved as fast as a man can run. South Side residents raced ahead of the blaze. The people hoped they could cross the south branch of the Chicago River and reach safety downtown. Surely, they thought, the fire could not leap over the river. Bridges spanning the river became a nightmare of terror and noise. Men, women, and children—as well as horses and carts—scrambled toward

Above: For many years, most people believed that the Great Chicago Fire started when Mrs. Patrick O'Leary's cow kicked over a lantern in the barn.

Right: The Randolph Street Bridge was mobbed by terrified Chicagoans trying to escape the flames.

safety. Roaring like thunder, the fire pushed its way to the river. It sent a storm of red-hot cinders raining across the waters onto the rooftops downtown. In minutes, downtown was ablaze.

A newspaper editor named Horace White described the scene, "The dogs of hell were upon the housetops of La Salle Street. . . . A column of flame would shoot up from a burning building, catch the force of the wind, and strike the next [building]. It was simply indescribable in its terrible grandeur."

Near State Street, another man reported, "Horses, maddened by the heat and noise, and irritated by the falling sparks, neighed and screamed in fright and anger. . . . Dogs ran hither and thither, howling dismally." One mother said, "I fled with my children clinging to me, fled literally in a shower of fire."

For 24 hours, the fire raged unchecked. Finally, rain dampened its fury. Amid the smoke and ashes, Chicagoans counted their losses. Some 300 people were killed, 100,000 were made homeless, and $200 million in property was destroyed. Shocked by the disaster, poet John Greenleaf Whittier wrote,

Men clasped each other's hands and said
"The City of the West is dead."

Charred wood

This view of one section of the city shows the terrible effects of the Great Chicago Fire of 1871.

UP FROM THE ASHES

But, of course, Chicago was not dead. The terrible Chicago Fire was still smoking when a real estate agent placed a sign above the wreckage of his office: ALL GONE BUT WIFE, CHILDREN, AND ENERGY. A reporter from the *Chicago Evening Post* wrote, "When the fire was baffled, citizens who had cowered and fled before it arose bravely and said, 'We can conquer everything.' "

A building boom began as soon as the ashes of the old city cooled. In the span of months, new fire-resistant brick buildings bloomed. City government compelled builders to adhere to a strict fire code. The pace of construction was astonishing. In 1874, a British visitor walked on State Street and reported, "It is difficult to realize the fact that the busy thoroughfare with its beautiful buildings . . . was but three years before a heap of charred ruins."

Columbian Exposition tickets

What's in a Name? The Windy City

Most visitors believe Chicago got its nickname, the "Windy City," because of the constant—and sometimes ferocious—winds that blow in off the lake. In truth, New York City newspaper writers invented the name when the two cities fought over the right to host the World's Columbian Exposition of 1893. At that time, Chicago leaders argued so vociferously for the fair that New York writers called them the "windy politicians of Chicago." Hence came the name Windy City.

Flags waved and bands blared on May 1, 1893, as the city opened the World's Columbian Exposition. The World's Fair celebrated the 400th anniversary of Columbus's arrival in America.

Fairgoers marveled at newfangled devices such as refrigeration machines and motorized fire trucks. Architect and city planner Daniel Burnham designed the fairgrounds. Guests walked amid great white buildings, beside a lagoon, and over broad causeways.

The exposition opened 22 years after the Chicago fire, and not a trace of damage from the conflagration could be seen anywhere. The World's Fair was final proof that Chicago, like the mythical phoenix, had risen out of its own ashes.

ARCHITECTURE, LEGACY OF THE FIRE

In the years after the Chicago Fire, hordes of young architects flocked to Chicago. The architects found excitement in the prospect of rebuilding a whole city. The post-fire period also coincided with two architectural developments: the elevator, and iron or steel framing. Steel allowed architects to build a tall skeleton to serve as a building's framework. Elevators made multistoried structures practical. The result was the skyscraper, Chicago's gift to world architecture. The world's first skyscraper was the ten-story Home Insurance Building, built in downtown Chicago in 1884.

Architect William Le Baron Jenney designed the Home Insurance Building. Jenney also helped to create a new architectural style called the "Chicago School." Architects influenced by the

Architect William Le Baron Jenney (above) designed the world's first skyscraper, Chicago's Home Insurance Building.

Right: An 1890s Chicago street scene

Chicago School based their buildings on steel frameworks. Outer walls were called "curtain walls" because they were thin and did not act to hold the building up. Such steel frameworks allowed architects to create wide glass windows. Consequently, Chicago's newest structures leaped to great heights, yet they looked light and graceful.

Chicago School architects often adorned their buildings with iron or masonry ornaments. A stunning example of such ornamentation can be found on the Carson Pirie Scott department store, built in the 1890s by architect Louis H. Sullivan.

The beautiful cast-iron floral panels that adorn the Carson Pirie Scott Building (right) were designed by Chicago architect Louis H. Sullivan. The Transportation Building (below) was Sullivan's contribution to the 1893 World's Columbian Exposition.

Frank Lloyd Wright was another architect with revolutionary ideas who came to Chicago during the post-fire period. Wright concentrated on designing houses. His greatest Chicago monument is the Robie House (1909), a breathtaking example of his "Prairie School" of architecture. The long and narrow Robie House flowed harmoniously into the prairie flatlands that dominated the city.

Above: Frank Lloyd Wright designed the Heurtley House in Oak Park.

Right: Chicago's Robie House, one of Wright's famous "prairie-style" houses

The twin glass buildings on Lake Shore Drive (in the center of this picture) are considered the masterpieces of architect Ludwig Mies van der Rohe.

Wright lived and worked in the Chicago suburb of Oak Park from 1889 to 1909. Marvelous examples of his houses remain in that suburb.

The Chicago contribution to architecture did not end in the post-fire era. In the 1940s, German-born Ludwig Mies van der Rohe started a second school of Chicago architecture. His apartment-house towers on Lake Shore Drive are symphonies of glass and steel. Van der Rohe subscribed to the "less is more" philosophy of design. He left the outside walls of his buildings free of decoration.

Helmut Jahn was the city's principal architect of the 1980s and 1990s. Jahn's bold State of Illinois Building is a landmark in the heart of the Loop. New buildings, standing beside the early skyscrapers, reaffirm that Chicago is a world leader of twentieth-century architecture.

Hog Butcher for the World,

Tool Maker, Stacker of Wheat,

*Player with the Railroads and
    the Nation's Freight Handler,*

Stormy, husky, brawling,

City of the Big Shoulders . . .

Carl Sandburg, *Chicago*

Chicago gained its fame and its riches through industry. For generations, it was a factory town, known for its grit and its smokestacks. But Chicago also enjoyed a lively cultural life. The town's writers, musicians, artists, and sports heroes made it one of the most exciting of the world's great cities.

BIRTH OF THE BLUES

It is sometimes said, "You have to know the blues in order to sing them." Consider a famous song by Chicago blues artist McKinley Morganfield, better known as Muddy Waters. The song tells of a man's love for his sweetheart. The sweetheart rejects his love. The man cries out, "I got my mo-joe workin', but it just don't work on you." Sadness. The musical expression of sadness lies at the heart of the blues.

Certainly, the African Americans of Chicago understood sadness. Great masses of African Americans came to Chicago from the segregated South during World War I and again during World War II. Like other immigrants, they hoped to find good jobs in the factories and good homes in the neighborhoods. Chicago seemed to them the Biblical Promised Land. Instead, they discovered that many factories routinely turned away African American job seekers. They were also unwanted in most neighborhoods. African Americans were forced to crowd into the slums of the South Side.

The Promised Land became a city of frustration. But from the South, the African Americans brought jazz and its cousin, a form of music loosely called "the blues." The driving beat of the blues throbbed with disappointment and anger. Yet the music offered a kernel of hope. One old song said, "But I won't be blue always/ You know the sun, the sun gonna shine/ In my back door some day." In the 1920s, Chicago became the world capital of blues music. Joe "King" Oliver led the hottest jazz and blues band of the era.

By 1936, jazz trumpeter Louis Armstrong was famous the world over.

The key player in Oliver's band was Louis "Satchmo" Armstrong. Armstrong and Oliver played in blues clubs that were concentrated on the South Side.

A classic Chicago-style blues band features a singer backed by a harmonica, a drum, and an electric guitar.

Today, scores of such bands play in blues clubs throughout the city. The music appeals to people of all backgrounds. Modern Chicago blues artists include Koko Taylor and Buddy Guy. Blues is music that comes from the very soul of "Sweet Home Chicago."

Top: A favorite Chicago jazz club is Andy's, where patrons never know which famous musicians might show up to sit in.
Right: Musicians at the annual Grant Park Blues Festival

THE WRITERS

Poet Carl Sandburg called Chicago the "City of the Big Shoulders." Novelist Nelson Algren called it the "City on the Make." Chicago writers never tire of defining their city. And they delight in telling stories with Chicago's streets and alleys in the background.

Writer James T. Farrell was popular in the 1930s and 1940s. The hero of Farrell's books was a young tough from the South Side named Studs Lonigan. A furious street fighter, Lonigan both shocked and fascinated readers. Nelson Algren wrote stories about working people who haunted the bars and gambling dens of the North Side. Algren's stories are not pretty, nor do they have happy endings. Instead, his stories reflect their settings—mean streets, desperate people.

Chicago's African-American writers found fame in the years after World War II. Willard Motley's book *Knock on Any Door* was a bestseller in the late 1940s. Motley was an African-American man from Chicago. He realized that few publishers of his era would buy a novel with an African-American central character. So Motley created a white hero in Nick Romano, a misunderstood Italian criminal from the West Side slums.

Gwendolyn Brooks is an award-winning poet who grew up in an African-American neighborhood called Bronzeville. Her first book of poems was called *A Street in Bronzeville* (1945).

Poet Carl Sandburg called Chicago the "City of the Big Shoulders."

Left: Nelson Algren, author of The Man with the Golden Arm *and* A Walk on the Wild Side, *is one of Chicago's most-famous native sons.*

Below: Gwendolyn Brooks, 1968 Poet Laureate of Illinois, spends much of her time nurturing young Chicago poets.

In 1968, Brooks became the Poet Laureate of Illinois. "I want [my] poems to be free," she said. "I want them to be direct without sacrificing the kinds of music, the picture making I've always been interested in."

Chicago is a newspaper town. One of the city's most popular newsmen is Mike Royko of the *Chicago Tribune.* Royko enjoys exposing crooks in city government. But he also tells stories based on a made-up character named Slats Grobnik. According to Royko, Slats grew up in a typical Chicago working-class neighborhood:

"A second-floor apartment above a tavern with the L tracks in the back." Like many kids, Slats loved summer vacation and loathed returning to school. "Nobody dreaded going back to school more than Slats," wrote Royko. "He couldn't stand being cooped up all day. His wild free spirit was meant to roam the wide-open alleys. . . . Also, he did not believe in getting up before noon."

THE SPORTING LIFE

The Daley Center in the middle of the Loop has a large plaza. In 1967, workers erected a 50-foot-tall metal sculpture in the plaza. The sculpture was designed by the famous Spanish artist Pablo Picasso. Art critics claimed the work was profound. But a city alderman took one look at the sculpture and said, "It ought to be torn down and replaced by a statue of Ernie Banks." Banks was an immensely popular baseball player with the Chicago Cubs. The love of sports is so great in this city that many people agreed with the alderman. They would rather have the statue of a baseball player gracing their plaza than a work by Picasso.

A passion for sports begins at a young age. Chicago residential neighborhoods have alleys running behind the buildings. The alleys are supposed to be places to park cars or to put garbage containers. But for working-class children, alleys double as sports fields. A rusting hoop bolted high on a garage serves as a basketball court. A strike zone painted on a brick wall is a field for a makeshift baseball game called "fast pitch." Fast pitch often involves only three players: a pitcher, a fielder, and a batter.

Sixteen-inch softball is a game unique to Chicago. It is played with a softball measuring 16 inches in circumference. The rest of the country uses the 12-inch variety. No gloves are worn by fielders in the Chicago game.

Softball is only one of the many sports activities and other programs available at parks throughout the city.

In 16-inch softball, the pitcher must pitch the ball underhand and slowly. Just about any hitter can clobber the ball in a 16-inch contest. But this means that fielders must be ever alert to run down fly balls and snag line drives. Special rules apply when pick-up games are played with fragments of a team. The rules are usually made up on the field. No right fielder? No problem. A drive to right field is an automatic out. No first baseman means, "Pitcher's hands are out."

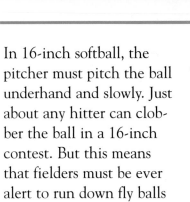

Top: Beach volleyball on the shores of Lake Michigan
Right: A 16-inch softball

Michael Jordan. Frank "Big Hurt" Thomas. Ryne Sandburg. Walter Payton. Gale Sayers. Bobby Hull. All these men are Chicago sports heroes. In 1996, an advertiser put up a billboard of a Bulls basketball star wearing a certain brand of suit. The billboard faced the city's busy Kennedy Expressway. After just a few days, the advertiser had to take the billboard down. Drivers slowing down to gape at the picture caused massive traffic jams. Great players are idolized in the city. Some open businesses such as restaurants and car dealerships. Because of the stars' popularity on the field, the businesses are overrun with customers. And why not adore sports heroes? Great players make for great teams. The Chicago Bulls of the 1990s, led by superstar Michael Jordan, was one of the strongest pro basketball teams in history.

And then there are baseball's Chicago Cubs.

According to legend, the owner of a restaurant and tavern tried to attend a Cubs game in 1945. He brought his

Michael Jordan, one of history's greatest athletes, led the Chicago Bulls in the 1990s.

Ernie Banks

In the 1950s and early 1960s, the Cubs were clearly the most dismal team in baseball. But they had one hero—Ernie Banks. Affectionately called "Mr. Cub," Banks was a sharp hitter with plenty of home-run power. He was named the National League's Most Valuable Player in both 1958 and 1959. He was popular with the fans because of his sunny personality and his genuine enthusiasm for baseball. His favorite expression was, "Let's play two," meaning the Cubs should play a double-header every game day.

There's always a crowd at the "Friendly Confines of Wrigley Field" on game days, even though the Cubs haven't won a World Series in more than fifty years.

pet billy goat with him on a leash. He was turned away by an usher. No goats allowed. The restaurant owner put a curse on the team. "You Cubs will never win another world championship," he growled. Thus, the Cubs were doomed for the next fifty years. From 1945 to 1995, they failed to win a single world pennant. No other team in American sports owns such a record of futility. The Cubs fielded their finest team in 1969, and that squad finished second to the New York Mets. Still, Cub fans flock to what they call the "Friendly Confines of Wrigley Field." It is a comfortable, old ballpark—one where grandparents like to take their grandchildren. And who knows? Perhaps some day the curse of the billy goat will be lifted.

Exuberant Cub announcer Harry Caray is one of Chicago's favorite people.

A line in the Chicago song goes, "Bet your bottom dollar you'll lose the blues in Chicago, Chicago . . ." *Blues* in this case means "boredom." The line is correct. A visitor to Chicago is rarely bored. The city offers hundreds of exciting things to do and places to see.

MUSEUMS

The Museum of Science and Industry is Chicago's most-visited institution. It is a fantasy land of whirling motors, spacecraft, and other items touched by science. Some 2,000 exhibits are displayed in 75 major halls. Popular attractions include a working coal mine, the world's largest model train, a German submarine captured in World War II, a working model of a human heart large enough to walk through, and an incredible dollhouse built like a fairy castle.

Reconstructions of great dinosaurs are a prime presentation at the Field Museum of Natural History. Nearby is the John G.

Left: This huge model of a human heart at the Museum of Science and Industry is large enough to walk through.
Below: The German submarine U-505 is displayed on the grounds of the museum.

THE GIANT HEART

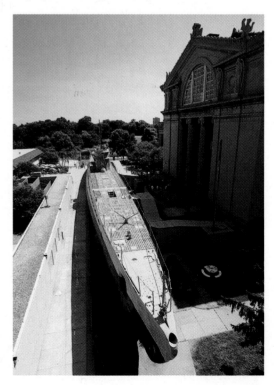

Shedd Aquarium. The largest aquarium in the world, it has 200 fish tanks holding more than 7,000 species of fish. Several tanks present the amazing variety of fish found in Chicago's very own Lake Michigan. The Shedd Aquarium's latest addition is the Oceanarium. Built to replicate the Pacific Northwest, the Oceanarium has sea otters and beluga whales. A genuine moon rock and models of the solar system are highlights at the Adler Planetarium. Images of the heavens are presented in fascinating sky shows.

Above: A dinosaur skeleton at the Field Museum
Right: Dolphin-feeding time at the Oceanarium

The Chicago Art Institute is one of the world's great art museums. Works there range from early Japanese prints to the latest in American art. Experts claim the Chicago museum holds the finest collection of French Impressionist paintings that can be found anywhere. History comes alive at the Chicago Historical Society. One especially moving diorama shows the city skyline in 1871, with the flames of the Chicago Fire raging above the buildings.

Chicago enjoys celebrating its rich ethnic heritage. Popular fairs and festivals honor such dates as Mexican Independence Day, Chinese New Year, Columbus Day

Children at the Art Institute examining Gustave Caillebotte's 1876 huge painting titled Paris, a Rainy Day

Chicago museums regularly feature activities for children.

(Italian), Octoberfest (German), and everyone's favorite—St. Patrick's Day (Irish). The Bud Billiken Parade, held in late summer, is dedicated to the young African-American people of Chicago. The city also supports a host of ethnic museums. African-American heritage is the theme of the Du Sable Museum of African American History. The Mexican Fine Arts Museum welcomes visitors into the brilliant world of Mexican painting. Folk art and Polish American art are displayed at the Polish Museum of America. Exhibits there remind guests that the Chicago area holds the largest concentration of Polish people found anywhere outside of Warsaw.

Left: July Fourth fireworks in the harbor off Grant Park
Right: Students at Chicago's Keller School

MONUMENTS TO THE PAST

About 14 miles south of the Loop lies a neighborhood called Pullman Village. In the 1880s it was a factory town built by industrialist George Pullman. Pullman earned a fortune manufacturing railroad sleeping-cars. His village had tree-lined streets with neat rows of apartment buildings, a church, a hotel, and a central market. But Pullman charged his workers high rents to live in his ideal town. An economic depression in 1893 caused Pullman to cut wages and fire factory workers. He did not lower rents. The result was the great Pullman Strike, one of the most violent labor battles in American history. Today, Pullman Village is a pleasant place to live.

The 1894 railway strike was one of the most violent labor battles in American history.

The Florence Hotel in Pullman Village as it looks today

On December 2, 1942, a team of scientists led by physicist Enrico Fermi gathered beneath the football stands of the University of Chicago. A nuclear reactor had been built secretly there. That day, the scientists achieved the first controlled nuclear chain reaction. This process was a vital step in making the atomic bomb. Chicago has since had the dubious honor of being the birthplace of nuclear weapons. A sculpture by Henry Moore called *Nuclear Energy* now marks the historic spot.

Above: Henry Moore's sculpture Nuclear Energy *at the University of Chicago*
Below: The University of Chicago campus

A bronze sculpture called *Pillar of Fire* stands on the ground where the Chicago Fire started in 1871. In the background is the Chicago Fire Academy, where the city trains its beginning firefighters. The Water Tower on North Michigan Avenue is a survivor of the Chicago Fire. Built in 1869, the castlelike tower is a famous Chicago landmark. Near the Michigan Avenue Bridge, historical markers note the place where Fort Dearborn was built in 1803. Fort Dearborn was the first building of substance erected on the site of Chicago.

On the North Side stands the Biograph Theater. It is a symbol of the past that many Chicagoans would like to forget. In 1934, bank robber John Dillinger was shot and killed by government agents as he left the Biograph after a movie. The killing was one of many bloody incidents from Chicago's crime-filled period of the 1920s and 1930s. Another famous mobster of the era was Al Capone, who operated an

Left: The Pillar of Fire sculpture stands on DeKoven Street at the very spot where the Great Chicago Fire of 1871 started.
Right: This section of the Michigan Avenue Bridge is the site of the original Fort Dearborn. The marks at the lower left corner of the picture are partial outlines of the fort.

Bank robber John Dillinger (right) was killed by government agents outside the Biograph Theater (left) in 1934.

Al Capone (below) was the most-famous Chicago mobster of the 1920s and 1930s.

illegal booze empire in the city. Crime sprees of the 1920s and 1930s forever gave Chicago the reputation of a wide-open gangland town. Today, politicians point out that Chicago has a low crime rate compared to other big American cities. But many Chicagoans feel a sort of perverse pride in the gang-land era. For decades after Dillinger's death, boys played "cops-'n'-robbers" outside the Biograph Theater. All the boys wanted to play the role of John Dillinger; not one of them wanted to be a law-enforcement man.

DOWNTOWN HAPPENINGS

Four of the world's ten tallest buildings stand in downtown Chicago. Chicagoans enjoy pointing out these structures to outsiders. They even create nicknames for the giants. The John Hancock Building is "Big John"; the Standard Oil Building is "Big Stan." Residents once boasted having the tallest of them all—the 110-story Sears Tower. Completed in 1974, Sears Tower was king of world skyscrapers. Then, in 1996, an office building was completed in Malaysia that was slightly taller than Sears Tower. No longer did the city have bragging rights to the world's tallest building. Many people were saddened at being overshadowed by a foreign skyscraper. But Chicagoans have always bounced back from disappointments. Think of the Fire.

Think of the Cubs.

For 22 years, Sears Tower (left) was the tallest building in the world.

Navy Pier, once used as a navy training base, has been completely refurbished and now boasts a children's museum, a glass-walled grand ballroom, restaurants, shops, a carousel, and a lighted Ferris wheel (right).

The Man on Five

The Daley Center is named for Richard J. Daley, who was mayor from 1955 until his death in office in 1976. No other mayor in the city's history held the seat longer. After Daley's death came a series of spirited and even bitter elections. In 1979, Chicago's first woman mayor, Jane Byrne, was elected. Four years later, Byrne was defeated by Harold Washington, the first African-American mayor. In 1989, Richard M. Daley, the son of Richard J. Daley, was elected mayor of Chicago. The mayor's office is on the fifth floor of City Hall, across the street from the Daley Center. Because of the fifth-floor location, political insiders often refer to the mayor as "The Man on Five."

These Lake Michigan boaters have a spectacular view of the John Hancock Building, which towers above its neighboring skyscrapers.

A souvenir paperweight of the Chicago skyline

Touring the city's outdoor sculptures is a popular downtown pastime. Queen of the Loop's sculpture show is the Chicago "Picasso," located at the Daley Center Plaza. An eternal question is asked and never answered: What does the "Picasso" represent? Some claim the statue looks like the face of a woman. Visitors are invited to study it and make their own interpretations. One of the city's best-loved outdoor artworks is the glass-and-stone mosaic called *Four Seasons*. Created by artist Marc Chagall, the work depicts the seasons' passage from spring to winter and the transition of human beings from infancy to old age. An interesting steel beam sculpture by Alexander Calder called *The Flamingo* seems poised to fly away from its downtown plaza. On the western end of the Loop stands *Batcolumn*, a steel sculpture by Claes Oldenberg that is shaped like a giant baseball bat.

Free music shows are another downtown happening. Classical music is offered once a week at the city's old library (now the Cultural Center). Folk music and poetry readings are presented at the new Harold Washington Library. In the summer months, office workers enjoy eating their lunches outdoors. The First National Bank Plaza and the Daley Center Plaza hold regular band concerts to entertain lunchtime crowds.

The Petrillo Band Shell in Grant Park presents outdoor concerts with a full symphony orchestra on summer nights.

Artist Pablo Picasso never gave a name to this sculpture at the Daley Center Plaza.

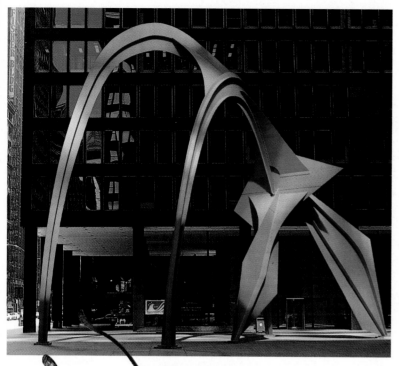

Grant Park also hosts popular blues, jazz, and gospel festivals.

Standing as the centerpiece of Grant Park is Buckingham Fountain. It welcomes and it bids farewell to many Chicago visitors. Including the metropolitan area, more than seven million people call this city by the lake their home. A popular blues song says this best:

Hello, baby, don't you

want to go

To that same ol' place

Sweet home, Chicago.

Above: The Flamingo, *by Alexander Calder*
Right: Buckingham Fountain

A dessert of sweet cherries tops off a brown-bag lunch eaten to the music of a band concert.

FAMOUS LANDMARKS

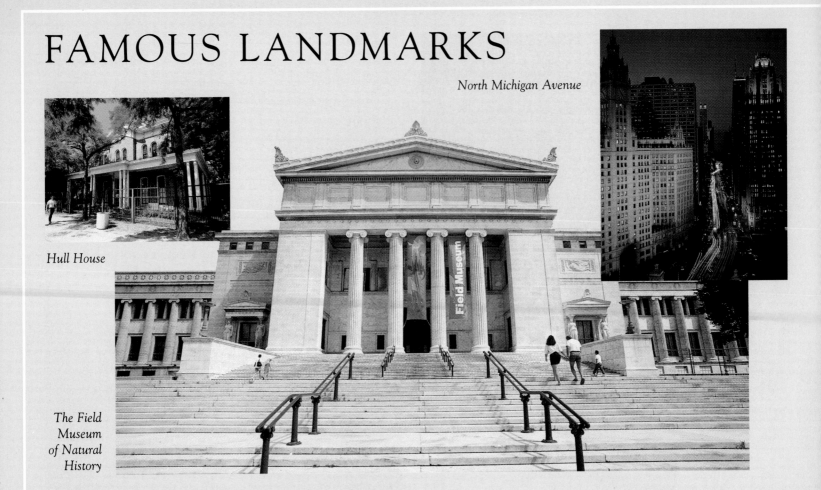

North Michigan Avenue

Hull House

Field Museum

The Field
Museum
of Natural
History

Grant Park
Downtown's major park, it holds the Buckingham Fountain and the world-famous Chicago Art Institute.

Museum Campus
The Field Museum of Natural History, the Adler Planetarium, and the John G. Shedd Aquarium are all located in one lakefront complex just south of downtown.

Outdoor Sculpture
The Chicago "Picasso" is in the Daley Center Plaza; the *Flamingo* is in the Federal Building Plaza;

the *Four Seasons* is in the First National Bank Plaza; the *Batcolumn* is at 600 West Madison.

The Carson Pirie Scott Building
The ornate ironwork on this State Street department store was created by architect Louis Sullivan.

The Board of Trade Building
Each working day, millions of dollars of wheat and other farm products are exchanged in this building, located in the La Salle Street financial district.

Orchestra Hall
This concert hall on Michigan Avenue is home to the Chicago Symphony Orchestra, one of the world's finest.

The Magnificent Mile
This shopping and tourist area on Michigan Avenue north of the Chicago River is popular with Chicagoans and out-of-town guests. During the Christmas holiday season, the trees on this stunning boulevard are adorned with glittering Italian lights.

North Lake Shore Drive
The row of glimmering apartment buildings that tower over the lake house Chicago's elite.

The Gold Coast
Just west of Lake Shore Drive, the Gold Coast is a ten-square-block neighborhood of fashionable apartments, restaurants, and shops.

Old Town
A redeveloped residential neighborhood, it is famed for theaters, restaurants, and nightclubs.

Left: The Art Institute of Chicago
Below left: The Picasso sculpture

The College of the University of Chicago

Lincoln Park
Chicago's favorite playground, the park contains beaches, a conservatory, and the world-famous Lincoln Park Zoo.

O'Hare International Airport
The world's busiest airport lies on Chicago's far Northwest Side.

The University of Illinois at Chicago
This four-year branch of the University of Illinois system just west of the Loop serves thousands of Chicago's college students.

Hull House
The one-time headquarters of social work pioneer Jane Addams, Hull House is now a museum devoted to her work.

Greek Town
Along Halsted Street just west of the Loop is a row of Greek restaurants popular with Loop office workers.

The United Center
Home of the Chicago Bulls and the Chicago Blackhawks, this new stadium is a focal point for West Side housing redevelopment.

Garfield Park Conservatory
This conservatory boasts five acres of plants and flowers inside one of the largest greenhouses in the world.

Chinatown
The city's best Chinese restaurants are found in this small neighborhood just southwest of the Loop.

Pilsen
Known as "Little Mexico," it is a neighborhood of genuine Mexican restaurants and shops.

Museum of Science and Industry
Space and engineering are among the many themes touched in this, the city's most-visited museum.

University of Chicago
The university is renowned throughout the world as a center for scholarship.

FAST FACTS

POPULATION   1990

City: 2,783,726

Metropolitan Area: 7,500,000

For most of the twentieth century, Chicago was called the Second City because it was second to New York as the nation's most-populous city. By the 1990 census, however, Chicago was eclipsed by Los Angeles. Chicago is now the third largest city in the nation.

AREA   **City of Chicago:**   228 square miles

LOCATION   Chicago lies in northern Illinois, near the tip of Lake Michigan; this position puts the city in the heart of the American Midwest.

NEIGHBORHOODS   Chicago is made up of a downtown section, called the Loop, and three major residential neighborhoods: the North Side (north of the Loop), the West Side (west of the Loop), and the South Side (south of the Loop).

CLIMATE   Chicago has rugged winters and hot, muggy summers. The city and its surrounding lands are flat, allowing winds to whip through the neighborhoods. The average January temperature is 25 degrees Fahrenheit; the average July temperature is 75 degrees Fahrenheit.

INDUSTRIES   Years ago, the Chicago Stockyards made the city, in the words of Carl Sandburg, "The Hog Butcher of the World." The stockyards have moved, but Chicago is still the nation's leader in manufacturing food products. There are more than 14,000 factories in the Chicago metropolitan area. In addition to food products, the city produces iron and steel, electrical machinery, and chemicals. Chicago is connected to the Atlantic Ocean via the St. Lawrence Seaway; the seaway makes it an important international seaport. Chicago's O'Hare Airport is the world's busiest.

CHRONOLOGY

1782
Jean Baptiste Point du Sable builds a cabin along the Chicago River in the early 1780s; he resides in the Chicago region for the next 20 years

1803
The U.S. Government builds a small military post called Fort Dearborn near the mouth of the Chicago River at Lake Michigan

1812
About 50 settlers are killed and Fort Dearborn is burned during a battle called the Fort Dearborn Massacre

1816
Fort Dearborn is rebuilt

1837
Chicago has some 4,000 residents, and is incorporated as a city

1870
Chicago's population nears 300,000 people

1871
The Chicago Fire destroys much of the city, killing 300 people, and leaving 100,000 homeless

1889
Jane Addams, a pioneer social worker, establishes Hull House in an impoverished Chicago immigrant neighborhood

1893
Chicago hosts the World's Columbian Exposition

1900
In a spectacular engineering feat, the Chicago River is reversed so that it flows out of Lake Michigan

Summer fun on a Lake Michigan beach

1929
During what is called the "St. Valentine's Day Massacre," members of Al Capone's gang gun down seven rivals at a North Side garage; the incident establishes Chicago's image as a city of gangland violence during the 1920s

1933
The World's Fair, called A Century of Progress, is held on the Chicago lakefront

1942
The first controlled nuclear chain reaction, a vital step in making the atomic bomb, is achieved in Chicago

1968
A year of riots: African-American neighborhoods erupt after the assassination of Dr. Martin Luther King, Jr.; demonstrators clash with police at the Democratic National Convention

1987
Harold Washington, the city's first African-American mayor, dies in office

1991
Richard M. Daley, son of long-time mayor Richard J. Daley, is elected mayor of Chicago

1992
The Chicago River breaks into an old and unused tunnel system, flooding Loop basements, and causing millions of dollars worth of damage

1996
The Democratic National Convention is held in Chicago

CHICAGO

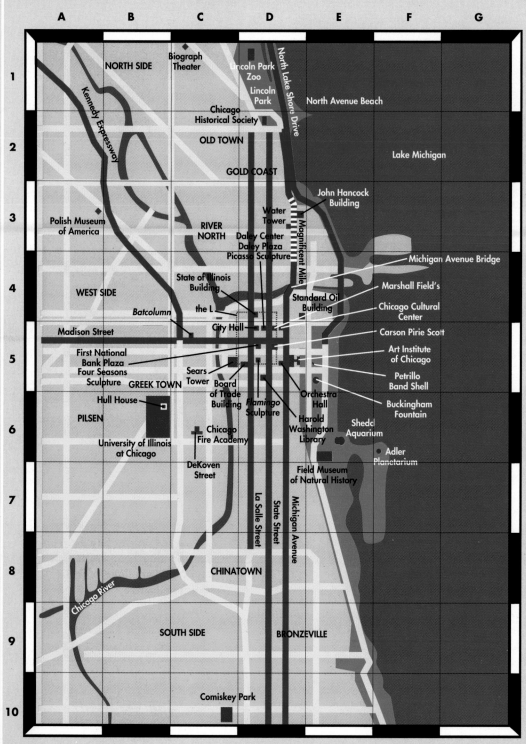

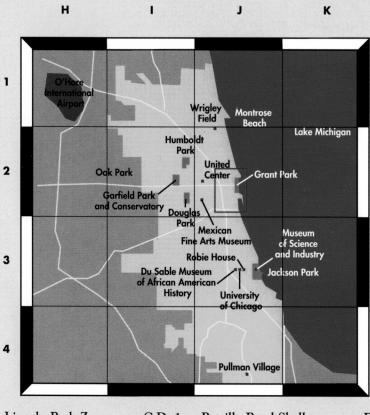

GLOSSARY

adorned: Decorated

booze: Slang term for alcoholic beverages

coincide: To occur at the same time as another event

conflagration: A great fire

depict: To represent, possibly by a picture or symbol

diorama: A three-dimensional scene usually displayed behind glass in a museum

exuberant: Full of life

futility: Uselessness

gruff: Rude or inconsiderate

harmonious: Blending in an agreeable and pleasing manner

laureate: Honored person

legacy: Lasting influence

loathed: Despised, hated

mosaic: A decorative design made of inlaid colored tiles

mythical: Not real; imaginary

perverse: Twisted or directed away from what is right

vociferously: Loudly, forcefully

Picture Identifications

Cover: Sears Tower and Chicago skyline; girl eating a hot dog; lion sculpture at the Art Institute of Chicago
Page 1: Friends and classmates at Chicago's Keller School
Pages 4-5: Buckingham Fountain's summertime light and color display
Pages 8-9: A view of the Chicago skyline from Chicago Harbor—from Sears Tower on the left to Lake Point Tower on the right
Pages 20-21: The Crosby Opera House in flames during the Great Chicago Fire of 1871
Pages 32-33: *The Four Seasons*, a mosaic sculpture by Marc Chagall in the First National Bank Plaza in downtown Chicago
Pages 42-43: The skyline of Chicago as seen from Oak Street Beach

Photo Credits

Cover (background), ©Peter Pearson/**Tony Stone Images, Inc.;** cover (left), ©**Cameramann International, Ltd.;** cover (right), ©**James P. Rowan;** 1, ©**The Futran Studio;** 3, ©KK&A, Ltd.; 4-5, ©Tom Firak/**mga/Photri;** 6, ©Tom Neiman/**First Image West, Inc.;** 7 (top left), ©J. Blank/**H. Armstrong Roberts;** 7 (middle right), ©Kevin O Mooney/**Odyssey/Chicago;** 7 (enchilada), ©KK&A, Ltd.; 8-9, ©**Cameramann International, Ltd.;** 9 (CTA tokens), ©KK&A, Ltd.; 10 (left), ©Robert Frerck/**Odyssey Productions;** 10 (right), ©Tom Neiman/**First Image West, Inc.;** 11 (left), ©Mark Segal/**Tony Stone Images, Inc.;** 11 (Frango Mints), ©KK&A, Ltd.; 12 (top), ©R. Kord/**H. Armstrong Roberts;** 12 (bottom), ©Camerique/**H. Armstrong Roberts;** 13 (top), ©P. Pearson/**H. Armstrong Roberts;** 13 (bottom), ©**Cameramann International, Ltd.;** 14 (top), ©Robert Frerck/**Odyssey Productions;** 14 (bottom), ©Paul Merideth/**Tony Stone Images, Inc.;** 15 (top left), ©Robert Frerck/**Odyssey/Frerck/Chicago;** 15 (top right), ©Robert Frerck/**Tony Stone Images, Inc.;** 15 (White Sox tickets), ©KK&A, Ltd.; 16 (left), ©P. Pearson/**H. Armstrong Roberts;** 16 (right), ©**The Futran Studio;** 17 (top left), ©Ron Schramm/**First Image West, Inc.;** 17 (bottom left), ©**The Futran Studio;** 17 (bottom right), ©**Brent Jones;** 18 (both pictures), ©**Brent Jones;** 19 (top), ©**Robert Holmes;** 19 (bottom), ©**The Futran Studio;** 20-21, Stock Montage, Inc.; 22 (both pictures), **Stock Montage, Inc.;** 23 (top), **The Bettmann Archive;** 23 (Water Tower sand sculpture), ©KK&A, Ltd.; 24 (top), **The Bettmann Archive;** 24 (bottom), **Stock Montage, Inc.;** 25 (charred wood), ©KK&A, Ltd.; 25 (bottom), **The Bettmann Archive;** 26 (World's Columbian Exposition tickets and World's Columbian Exposition souvenir card), ©KK&A, Ltd.; 27 (top), UPI/Bettmann; 27 (World's Columbian Exposition souvenir card), ©KK&A, Ltd.; 28 (top), ©**The Bettmann Archive;** 28 (bottom), Corbis-Bettmann; 29 (top), ©Tom Nieman/**First Image West, Inc.;** 29 (bottom), **Stock Montage, Inc.;** 30 (top), ©Mary A. Root/**Root Resources;** 30 (bottom), ©Tom Nieman/**First Image West, Inc.;** 31, ©**Cameramann International, Ltd.;** 32-33, ©Peter Pearson/**Tony Stone Images, Inc.;** 34, The Bettmann Archive; 35 (top), ©**Robert Holmes;** 35 (bottom), ©Zbigniew Bzdak; 36 (book), ©KK&A, Ltd.; 36 (right), **The Bettmann Archive;** 37 (top), **The Bettmann Archive;** 37 (bottom), UPI/Corbis-Bettmann; 38, ©**The Futran Studio;** 39 (top), ©Andre Jenny/**First Image West, Inc.;** 39 (softball), ©KK&A, Ltd.; 40 (top), ©Brian Drake/**mga/Photri;** 40 (bottom), UPI/Bettmann; 41 (left), ©S. Reed/**H. Armstrong Roberts;** 41 (right), ©**The Futran Studio;** 42-43, ©Steve Vidler/**SuperStock International, Inc.;** 44 (both pictures), ©**Cameramann International, Ltd.;** 45 (top), ©**Brent M. Jones;** 45 (bottom), ©**Dembinsky Photo Assoc.;** 46 (top), ©Robert Frerck/**Odyssey Productions;** 46 (bottom), ©**The Futran Studio;** 47 (left), ©**Cameramann International, Ltd.;** 47 (right), ©**The Futran Studio;** 48 (top), **The Bettmann Archive, Inc.;** 48 (bottom), ©Robert Frerck/**Odyssey/Frerck/Chicago;** 49 (top), ©**Cameramann International, Ltd.;** 49 (bottom), ©Camerique/**H. Armstrong Roberts;** 50 (both pictures), ©**Cameramann International, Ltd.;** 51 (top), UPI/Bettmann; 51 (right), **The Bettmann Archive;** 51 (bottom), **WideWorld Photos, Inc.;** 52 (left), ©Timothy Hursley/**SuperStock International, Inc.;** 52 (right), ©Zbigniew Bzdak; 53 (top left), ©**Cameramann International, Ltd.;** 53 (top right), **UPI/Corbis-Bettmann;** 53 (Chicago Skyline paperweight), ©KK&A, Ltd.; 54, ©**Cameramann International, Ltd.;** 55 (top), ©Robert Frerck/**Odyssey/Chicago;** 55 (bottom right), ©Michael Shedlock/**N E Stock Photo;** 55 (paper bag and cherries), ©KK&A, Ltd.; 56 (left and middle), ©**Cameramann International, Ltd.;** 56 (right), ©Mark Romine/**SuperStock International, Inc.;** 57 (top left), ©Matthew Kaplan/**mga/Photri;** 57 (right and bottom left), ©**Cameramann International, Ltd.;** 59, ©**Diana Rasche;** 60, ©KK&A, Ltd.; 61, ©KK&A, Ltd.

INDEX

Page numbers in boldface type indicate illustrations

TO FIND OUT MORE

BOOKS

Altman, Linda Jacobs. *The Pullman Strike of 1894: Turning Point for American Labor*. Brookfield, CT: Millbrook Press, 1994.

Aylesworth, Thomas G. *The Cubs*. New York: Gallery Books, 1990.

Basye, Ann. *Kids in the Loop: Chicago Adventures for Kids and Their Grown-Ups*. Chicago: Chicago Review Press, 1995.

Brooks, Philip. *Michael Jordan*. Chicago: Childrens Press, 1995.

Davis, James E. and Sharryl Davis Hawke. *Chicago*. Milwaukee: Raintree Publishers, 1990.

Davis, Lauren. *Kidding Around Chicago: A Young Person's Guide*. Santa Fe, NM: John Muir Publications, 1993.

Doherty, Craig A. *The Sears Tower*. Woodbridge, CT: Blackbird Press, 1995.

Harris, Bill. *Chicago: A Picture Memory*. Avenel, NJ: Crescent Books, 1994.

Murphy, Jim. *The Great Fire*. New York: Scholastic Inc., 1995.

Walker, Paul Robert. *Hoop Dreams*. Atlanta: Turner Publishing Inc., 1995.

ONLINE SITES

Art Institute of Chicago
http://www.artic.edu/aic/firstpage.html
Includes images from the famous Museum as well as historical information about Chicago

The Chicago Bulls
http://www.nba.com/bulls/
Official website for the most popular sports team in Chicago

Chicago Historical Society
http://www.chicagohs.org/
Extensive historical information and photos of Chicago as well as tours of current exhibits at the museum

Chicago Mosaic
http://www.ci.chi.il.us/
Official website for the City of Chicago; includes government information, city maps, history, schedules of events

Chicago Public Library
http://cpl.lib.uic.edu/CPL.html
In addition to library services, provides links to many other Chicago websites

Chicago Sun-Times
http://www.suntimes.com
Award-winning newspaper website, provides a wide variety of newsworthy information as well as connections to fun, interesting, and very cool Chicago, national, and international websites

Museum of Science and Industry
http://www.msichicago.org
Highlights some of the museum's most popular attractions, including a movie of a baby chick hatching, a tour of Colleen Moore's Fairy Castle, and a preview of upcoming Omnimax Theatre features

O'Hare International Airport
http://www.ci.chi.il.us/WorksMart/Aviation/OHare.html/
Information, terminal maps, photos, and history of the world's busiest airport

State of Illinois
http://www.state.il.us/
Explore Chicago and its neighboring communities on the official website of the State of Illinois

ABOUT THE AUTHOR

R. Conrad Stein was born and grew up in Chicago. After serving in the Marine Corps, he attended the University of Illinois and received a degree in history. He later lived and studied in Mexico. Mr. Stein has published many books for young readers. He now lives in Chicago with his wife and their daughter, Janna.

How much of a Chicagoan is Mr. Stein? While in the Marine Corps, an officer walked among his ranks asking each man where he was from. "New Jersey, sir!" one man said. "California, sir!" said another. All gave the name of their home state. When Mr. Stein's turn came, he said, "Chicago, sir!" His home state—Illinois—was a secondary consideration in his mind. He was and is a true Chicagoan.